HOLA little Lola

Spanish and English ABC
ABC en Inglés y Español

by Lucia Ciomei

ISBN-13: 978-0692823200

ISBN-10: 0692823204

This book is for my two bilingual princesses,
little Lola & baby Lía

Este libro es para mi dos princesas bilingües,
pequeña Lola y bebé Lía

A a

is for AIRPLANE

·······························

de AVIÓN

B b

is for BOAT
....
de BARCO

Cc

is for COOKING

······································

de COCINAR

Dd

is for DINOSAUR

de DINOSAURIO

Ee

is for ELEPHANT
···
de ELEFANTE

Ff

is for FLOWERS

de FLORES

G g

is for GUITAR

·······································

de GUITARRA

Hh

is for HELLO

....

de HOLA

I i

is for IMAGINATION
···
de IMAGINACIÓN

J j

is for JUICE

....

de JUGO

Kk

is for KILO

de KILO

Ll

is for LAMP

....

de LÁMPARA

M m

is for MOM
··
de MAMÁ

N n

is for NEW YORK

·····························

de NUEVA YORK

O o

is for OFFICE

· ·

de OFICINA

P p

is for PIANO

de PIANO

Q q

is for QUESADILLA

....

de QUESADILLA

Rr

is for ROBOT
....
de ROBOT

S s

is for SUN
....
de SOL

Tt

is for TAXI

de TAXI

U u

is for UNIVERSE
....
de UNIVERSO

V v

is for VOLCANO
....
de VOLCÁN

W w

is for WAFFLES
···
de WAFLES

X x

is for XYLOPHONE

de XILÓFONO

Yy

is for YOGA

de YOGA

Z z

is for ZOMBIE
··
de ZOMBI

www.ingramcontent.com/pod-product-compliance
Lightning Source LLC
Chambersburg PA
CBHW041054110426
42740CB00045B/132